RAINBOW SPLINTERS

A COLLECTION OF POEMS

PAUL PALMER

Copyright © 2024 Paul Palmer

The moral right of the author has been asserted.

Apart from any fair dealing for the purposes of research or private study, or criticism or review, as permitted under the Copyright, Designs and Patents Act 1988, this publication may only be reproduced, stored or transmitted, in any form or by any means, with the prior permission in writing of the publishers, or in the case of reprographic reproduction in accordance with the terms of licences issued by the Copyright Licensing Agency. Enquiries concerning reproduction outside those terms should be sent to the publishers.

Matador
Unit E2 Airfield Business Park,
Harrison Road, Market Harborough,
Leicestershire. LE16 7UL
Tel: 0116 2792299
Email: books@troubador.co.uk
Web: www.troubador.co.uk/matador
Twitter: @matadorbooks

ISBN 978 1 80514 178 5

British Library Cataloguing in Publication Data.
A catalogue record for this book is available from the British Library.

Printed and bound in Great Britain by 4edge Limited
Typeset in 11pt Minion Pro by Troubador Publishing Ltd, Leicester, UK

Matador is an imprint of Troubador Publishing Ltd

*Many thanks to my dear wife, Carol,
also the friends and family who have
encouraged and supported me.*

CONTENTS

Dawn	1
They Called It the Devil's Music	2
The Curse of COVID	4
Fox Gloves and Forget-Me-Nots	7
The Little Crab Catchers	8
The Shape of a Woman	10
Fred's Old Shed	11
Regret	13
No Names	14
Masters of Their Crafts	16
Storm at Dawn	19
Couch Potato	20
The Last Blast of the Trumpet	22
Sunset, Moonrise	24
Boats and Beach	25
The Wheelwright and the Candlemaker	26
The Poppy	28
Straight Trick	30
Revelation	32
Night Road	35
The Comparisons of Youth, Then and Now	36
Rings of the Rain	39
Mankind	41
The Web	42
Table for Two	44

Topless	46
Fire by Water	48
Childhood Street	50
Stray Tear	56
Heathcliff's Wife	57
The Waste of Worry	60
Friendship	61
The Feast of the Fairies	62
Dirty Dogs and Sour Flowers	64
Mist, Sea and Shore	67
Hands	68
Sit Dad in the Corner	71
Thirst for the First	74
A Pun-net of Tutti Frutti	75
The Right to Bear Arms	77
Dandelion	80
Hope	81
Pandora's Box	82
The Old Nostalgia Inn	84
Endless Soul	87
Black Mushrooms	88
Youth's Delicate Frame	89
Broken Heart	91
Bones in a Blanket	92
The Sound of the Sea	94
Eyewitness	95
Butterfly in the Rain	96
Dealer	97
Nature's Crowning Glory	98
The Highwayman	100
The Passing	103

Born to Be Mild	104
First Light	107
Alcohol, My Enemy or My Friend?	108
The Remnant of Life	111
Sleep	112
The Sun of Vesta and Ra	113
Love Birds	114
Trump 2018	115
Moon Beach	118
When	120
Rainbow Splinters	122
The Fortunes and Follies of Fame	123
It's Cool	125
Summer's Door	127
Tranquil Shadows	128

DAWN

The keen curved blade of the moon
Sliced through night's black canopy
And dawn spilled scarlet upon the earth
The stars like a billion shards of shattered glass
Were swept away like dust
And the sword of night was stilled
In its scabbard of blue.

Mountains appeared to roll and wrestle
With the shadow of restless cloud
And a multitude of green tongues
Whispered from the trees
As morning sighed
And breathed upon the land.

The long grass moved as an emerald
Cloak upon hills' shoulders
Embraced the crest and vale
In liquid flow
In slow motion
As it succumbed to still.

Cobweb pearls glisten betwixt twig and stem
As sun ascends to lay down oak's crooked shadow
A multi-fingered hand
Across the face of time
And so another day
In a trillion days begins.

THEY CALLED IT THE DEVIL'S MUSIC

They referred to us as delinquents
Tearaway teens that had sold their souls
They accused it of being the devil's music
But we called it rock and roll.

It began with Bill Haley in the *Blackboard Jungle*
With 'Rock Around the Clock'
Then came the Teddy Boys in drainpipe trousers
Drape jackets and luminous socks.

Little Richard ripping it up stomping on piano
Backed by a line-up of wailing saxophones
Elvis gyrating his pelvis in black leather
Filmed in crackling audio and monochrome.

The beautiful haunting voice of Roy Orbison
How could he be in the devil's choir?
His songs heaven-sent with emotion
And no octave in rock could be higher.

Then on that fateful February night
Three rock souls perished
Along with the plane and the crew
But the sound of Buddy Holly raves on through the ages
With the echoes of 'Peggy Sue'.

The harmony of the Everly Brothers
Gave us that wonderful feeling of being so young and free
Or the thrill of jiving in the cinema aisles to 'Great Balls of Fire'
From that wild rocker Jerry Lee.

We were there at the birth of the devil's music
It uplifted our spirits and did not steal our souls
And it will live on forever
And we call it rock and roll.

THE CURSE OF COVID

We thought we were cursed
In fear of our annihilation
When came the coronavirus
Invaded by an abomination.

We were told we must disinfect
Wash our hands to protect
And put ourselves into isolation
Some said it would be our ruination
The economy will go into free fall
And into stagnation.

Doctors and nurses
Plunged into danger without PPE
We were asking why
And 200,000 people about to die
They were under pressure
And frustration
That their patients
Could not get their treatments
And operations.

For the nurses we all cheered
Banging our saucepans
In confused ironic jubilation
Finding it hard to understand the situation
But the scientists were working to find a cure
To us the prospect seemed so obscure.

They said when we succeed
There will be a transformation
Hopefully then we will get our liberation
Then we were informed it had undergone a mutation
Now we had another variation.

Our saviour Professor Gilbert had finally arrived with
    the AstraZeneca vaccination
Now there was no time for procrastination
As Pfizer was on its way to our island nation.

Get in line no hesitation
The population in masked formation
Outside the surgeries
Emerging from hibernation.

We received our jabs
With relief and elation
To save the world
To protect the nation.

Now we live in hope
But also with a little trepidation
It's not yet time
For celebration
We now have war
Scandal and inflation
Underpaid nurses at food banks

In desperation
The old and the young
With unaffordable heating and deprivation.

At the very least let's salute
The hospital workers and the nurses
Give them a raise
After all the death and distress
They deserve our praise
Let's show some respect
To those who sacrificed their lives
For us and the NHS.

They rescued us from the COVID curse
They were our salvation
They were the brave few
That gave so many their liberation.

FOX GLOVES AND FORGET-ME-NOTS

The fox pulls on his gloves
When the snow drops
And the bluebells ring
As the dandy lion is crowned
The grass verge king.

Tulips sup
From the butter cup
Until the shepherd's purse is spent
And the dog rose
Understands the bark of the tree.

Ivy clings
When the cow slips
And from out of the blue
An anguished voice cries forth
Forget me not.

The bulbs of daffodils
Cast their golden light
Into the deadly night shade.

Where snap dragons
Snap at red hot pokers
And wisteria weeps with the willow
As love lies bleeding
On the blades of grass.

THE LITTLE CRAB CATCHERS

Along came
The little crab catchers
With their buckets
And some bacon rashers.

No phones or Game Boys
To spoil the time
As intently
They cast their lines.

The children content
In their simplicity
Completely void
Of any technology.

They cast their lines
On grasping claw
One after another
They cast for more.

As the kids with glee
Focused on bringing in their catch
No demands for ice cream
Sweets or cash.

No protest when it's time to go
Just cheers of joy and jubilation
As they release and repatriate
Their captive crustaceans.

Then with a fond farewell
Hand in hand with mums and dads
As they wave and say
"Bye bye crabs."

THE SHAPE OF A WOMAN

Anatomy was never so sublime
To draw the female body
With curving lines so fine
Each shadow cast
Beneath the crest
In wave of hair
Or swell of breast
In cleavage cleft
Of varied shade and sheen
No fantasy
Creates such a perfect dream.

FRED'S OLD SHED

Fred liked to tinker and potter in his shed
He knew where to find every screw, paint pot, brush
And even the odd turned rail
And on his bench with hammer and punch
He would countersink many a nail.

He could skilfully manipulate
A plane saw and file
And his timber was always stacked
In a neat orderly pile.

Sawdust and shavings
Lay pine-scented and spent upon the floor
His bib and brace overalls
Hung on the back of a paint-tested door.

There were boxes and jars and an old chest of drawers
Full of spanners, nuts, bolts, masking tape
And a ball of string
Tied up bundles of brass stair rods
Inside the coils of an old armchair spring.

Next to some sharp shiny chisels stood a sticky glue pot
With treacle-like run marks
Near an old battered tin
Full of G-Clamps, a paint-spattered mallet
And a discarded rusty bent panel pin.

Now who will oil the squeak
On the top hinge of the door?
For poor old Fred
Is with us no more.

With dust on his lathe
His shed stands silent and still
But at a glance there is a shadow of his ghost
From warm sunlight glinting on his old bench drill.

Now every item has been catalogued
The last lot is about to go under the hammer
In a crystal clear voice
With no hint of a stammer.

The slick auctioneer brings down his gavel
With a final smack
Sold to the gentleman
In the houndstooth cap.

REGRET

I cannot reverse time
And unravel the words that I have said
I cannot put them back in my mouth
I cannot take them out of your head.

To apologise and say the word 'sorry'
I know it is never enough
But if you knew the depth of my regret
It would surely melt away your rebuff.

NO NAMES

I know not your name
Yet I lie with you many times
We grip and slip, kiss and nip
Our flesh is one sometime.

Our tongues do not articulate
When I see you on that day
But they lick and kiss, our bodies talk
Whilst our loins in lust and expectations lay.

You roll into me
And warm the night
Only you know how to grasp me into you
And hold me tight.

Sheets tangle
And bind the limbs of you and me
Yet we kick and come
To be free.

Love moans and groans
With pleasured sighs
As I wish to dwell forever
Between your thighs.

Buttocks twitch
Eyes north to heaven bound
I cry with you
To soothe the sound.

But never let its rushing end
Yet in passion's throes in a spasm of heat
Endlessly its end
We seek.

Then you have gone, scarlet lips left
On your coffee cup
Leaving crumpled cotton across my thigh
Your crushed perfumed pillow and I
Alone to reflect and sigh.

MASTERS OF THEIR CRAFTS

The master of the tapestry
Illustrating with weaving thread
The sculptor carving stone and moulding clay
To shape the living and the dead.

The master carpenter
Turning his time upon the lathe
The stonemason
Etching script upon the grave.

The grave digger
Working in his consecrated hole
The vicar and the priest
The saviours of the soul.

The master swordsman
Who takes life with the blade
The master surgeon
With his blade a life he endeavours to save.

The artist at the easel
Creating the masterpiece
The politician's dilemma
As he tries to master war and peace.

The architect
The master of design
The master of calligraphy
The craftsman of the sign.

The draftsman
Drawing up the builder's plan
The master gardener
Nurturing seeds with a watering can.

The farmer
Raising cattle, pigs and sheep
Cultivating the land with crops
To plough, sow and reap.

The mechanic
The master of the car
The barrister and the publican
Both are masters at the bar.

The master of commerce
He needs your wallet and your purse
The writer and the poet
The master of chapter and verse.

The thespian
Who once was all the rage
Receiving Oscars from the film world
Standing ovations for his Hamlet on the stage.

The composer of the music
The player of the keys and strings
The conductor of the orchestra
When the choir sings.

They are all masters of their crafts
The weavers of the thread
The sculptors of life
Who shape and uplift the living and the dead.

STORM AT DAWN

Across the black clouded hills
Lightning lurched and screeched
With a deafening cry
As the crashing of a thunderbolt
Shot from a gun metal sky
Then the sun rose up
In a blood red stain
And the rain
Fell down with a sigh.

COUCH POTATO

I am a couch potato
I vegetate on my settee
Munching crisps and pizza
And slurping mugs of tea.

My vest is splattered with ketchup and egg stains
My shell suit bottoms shiny and tacky with grease
My belly hangs over the top of them
I think I might be obese.

I see the starving millions
On my widescreen TV
As into my mouth I sling some Cheesy Wotsits
And dunk jam doughnuts into my tea.

Then I cram in a bacon sandwich
After smothering it in melted cheese
Then I'll swig down some Diet Pepsi
Two burgers, a curry, chips and mushy peas.

Be-bar-be-bar-be-bar-be-bar
I'm now in intensive care
I've had a heart attack
Drips and tubes sticking out of me
I can't move laid upon my back.

I try to watch the monitor screen
I drift in and out of sleep
All I can hear is a *beep beep beep*
Beeeeeep.

THE LAST BLAST OF THE TRUMPET

The last blast of the trumpet,
We hear its clarion call,
As another old ale house,
Sadly closes its door.

Once Mrs Price dried her bloomers,
By the pub's open fire,
While skittles were played
In front of a window,
Protected by chicken wire.

With Jim behind the bar,
Our local curmudgeon,
With his droll wit,
Your senses he would bludgeon.

To ask for a gin and tonic,
With ice and a slice,
Was beyond the comprehension,
Of dear old Jim Price.

The last time the pub was painted,
Or had any form of decoration,
Was in 1953,
For the queen's coronation.

Hanging in the barn rafters,
Moth-eaten bunting, insisting to stay,
To remind a new generation,
Of a past celebrated day.

Once, after a game of bowls,
Having a pint and a chat,
In last week's resurrected sandwich,
Someone found an old beer mat.

A trip to the urinals,
Outside to the gents,
You would wash down with urine,
The pigeons' excrement.

Now it's goodbye to the fading past,
The hand pumps and the foaming beer,
The crisp hatch for the kids,
The bonhomie, the laughter, the cheer.

Goodbye to The Trumpet,
For hundreds of years, it opened its welcome doors,
Now this old ale house,
Is sadly no more.

SUNSET, MOONRISE

Running in the painted dust,
The embers of a twisting star,
Of scarlet and rust,
On horizon's broken ridge,
The light distorting,
On a golden bridge.

Quicksilver fragmented,
In the eastern sky,
Of speckled black,
Spills a golden disc,
From a clouded sack.

BOATS AND BEACH

Yachts with flapping flags and full-blown sails
Bobbing dinghies, boats, and fishermen's crafts
In a multitude of bright colours
And various draughts.

The sand is warm
The sea blue green and cool
Not hot and gritty
Like the paddling pool.

Ice cream drips
Off little pink hands
As they squat and build castles
From buckets of salty wet sand.

THE WHEELWRIGHT AND THE CANDLEMAKER

In the Dog and Gun they sat together,
The wheelwright and the candlemaker,
On an old beer-stained wooden table,
There was a fresh cottage loaf.
They both pulled at it with hungry relish.
Crumbs cascading onto the worn flagstone floor.
Also on the scarred, gnarled, uneven boards,
Stood a large jug of ale.
Foam sliding down the sides of two pewter tankards.
On a dish, some freshly churned butter and a large portion of homemade cheese.

After a busy day's work, secure in their knowledge,
For business was brisk for them both.
"One thing's for sure," said the wheelwright,
"People will always need wheels."
"Aye," said the candlemaker, "Happen you be right,
And to be sure, people will always need light."

Now! A car coughs into life.
The Dog and Gun still stands today,
With a large car park at the rear.
It now sells various lagers and beer.
The old table is still there,
Where the wheelwright and the candlemaker dined,
And dominoes they would play.
But the cheese has long been pasteurised away.

The landlord flashes the lights,
And calls time.
"Time, gentlemen, time!"

THE POPPY

Upon the fields of Flanders
The poppy brightly stands,
A vivid splash of scarlet,
On a quiet piece of land.

So many red poppies
Now sway in the fields of corn,
Bowing to a lost generation,
Now yet, another one is born.

Let them not forget the fallen
History should be well read,
For without its knowledge,
Ignorance again will count the dead.

So for the fading khaki
And also for the grey,
Stand for two minutes silence,
And for peace let us pray.

On the eleventh hour
Of the eleventh day,
In the cold chill of November,
An echo gun does bray.

The Armistice was signed
On that bitter winter day,
For the first time guns lay silent,
Bayonets broken in the clay.

The sounding of the last post
I hear the bugle blow,
For those mothers' sons now lie,
Where the poppies freely grow.

One frail old soldier
Recalls his comrades last stand,
And contemplates so many white crosses,
That saturate the land.

Once in that far-flung corner
The flower of youth did brightly stand,
Their splash of blood remembered,
Upon that quiet piece of land.

STRAIGHT TRICK

Her thigh boot heels
Were a staggering height
Her micro skirt
Was of the tightest white.

She wore a see-through top
And stockings of wide mesh black
And a shiny scarlet
Plastic mac.

Her bright pink lip gloss
Glistened in the neon light
As she emerged to the curb
This lady of the night.

She ducked her head and lewdly
Thrust her chest into the car
He asked how much
Said she, "Depends how far."

They reached a price
After a comprehensive list
But she said quite firmly
"You cannot kiss."

A deal was struck
She swung in her heels and hose
And slammed the passenger door
As exhaust fumes stung her nose.

They drove to a dark
And deserted lane
He was a quiet, gentle man
There was no fear of pain.

Post-coital blue-grey smoke
Inhaled in reflective silence
She was relieved
This time there was no violence.

REVELATION

COVID-19, is it nature's revenge?
Is it part of her design?
In the past so generous and bountiful
She has been so kind and benign.

Now she rises up
In anger and frustration
At melting glaciers, flood disasters
Raging fires and deforestation.

She has finally found
The clean air solution
To halt human arrogance and greed
To curb man's endless pollution.

With coronavirus she has arrested mankind
Put on hold in isolation
To purge the Earth
To prevent the planet's ruination.

In lockdown planes are grounded
While birds still take flight
Completely innocent and oblivious
To mankind's sorry plight.

Blossoms and wild flowers flourish
At the rebirth of spring
Birds building their nests
With their mating calls they sing
But the cry of humanity
Has a hollow ring.

Day by day
Freedom diminishes and dwindles
While cloistered inside
On computers, phones or Kindles.

Let out for a walk
Stay two metres apart
Do not tarry or overcrowd
The recreation grounds or the park.

Some venture outside
With fear and trepidation
Hoping one day for the all-clear
In anticipation.

Meanwhile it's gloves, masks
And plastic screens
Until we receive
That COVID vaccine.

Whilst in this dire situation
During our incarceration
Our fellow man comes forth
With hope, kindness, humour and cooperation.

Humankind I'm sure
One day will rise in unification
To prevent all living creatures
From annihilation.

Now the world must become
A one earth nation
We have been warned
Let 2020 be our vision, our revelation.

NIGHT ROAD

Along the night road
In haloes of swirling rain and sleet
Yellow orbs of lamplight
Suspended in the darkness of the street.

A paper bag flattened
By the rain
Awaits its partner
The morning wind
To make it dance again.

Drains they bare their teeth
And gargle with thirst so rare
Street stripped of your garbs of grime
The morning breaks once again
With the distant clock of sombre chime.

THE COMPARISIONS OF YOUTH, THEN AND NOW

On the back row on a Saturday night
Who cared about a film with a dull dialogue
When the main objective was a furtive fumble
And a tongue-wrestling snog.

You could hear those familiar sighs and moans
And the springs would groan and squeak
With couples groping in the darkness
In those old velvet cinema seats.

The dance halls packed to capacity
We would be jiving or doing the twist
We smoked, along with the rock bands
Unaware of our future health risks.

Panstick covered love bites
High lacquered beehives
Coffee bars with jukeboxes
Girls doing the hand jive.

We sang in the pubs around beer-soaked pianos
With nicotine-stained ceilings and blue hazy bars
We would all get blind drunk
And some would still drive their cars.

With full employment in factories and shops
We could swap and change without a care
For there was always plenty
Of jobs to spare.

Chatting up the girls you could get the brush off
Or a come on with a smile and a wink
But whatever the outcome
We would never ever spike their drinks.

A girl would feel safe
When she walked in the dark
When wolf whistling was a compliment
Or merely an innocent lark.

Now the young with their mobiles
On Twitter, YouTube or Facebook
Their digital dancing thumbs
Never seem still or off the hook.

I always thought the charm
Of an old-fashioned clock
Had a pleasing sound of calm
When it went tick-tock.

Now I find it's a moron
On a screen
Venting their spleen
And talking absolute rot.

Now it's unsocial media
Where invisible trolls and bullies hide and thrive
Inciting the storming of buildings
Causing grief and depression and sometimes suicide.

Yet, to the young it now seems strange
And somewhat deranged
But before pesticides
In the countryside.

Or the invasion of urban foxes
We, once went outside in winter squalls
To make telephone calls
In big bright red boxes.

RINGS OF THE RAIN

Swirling clouds
Staining horizons fading blues
Turning bleakly
Into tarnished silver-grey hues.

Out of the window
Tears on the pane
Sitting in dry comfort
Watching diamonds forming on frame.

Sheltered inside
I do like the sound
Of the constant splattering
Hearing it pound.

Blood shot reflections
Of cars slowing down
In acceleration
Red crystals vanish back into the ground.

Watching the interlocking
Rings of the rain
Accumulating on footpaths
In puddles again.

The wind gains confidence
From its early soft breeze
I can hear it
Aggressively stirring the trees.

Momentum gathers
It's almost enraged
The storm the tempest
With no restricting stage.

It performs
Wherever it wills
With thunderous crashing and lashing
From black nimbus it spills.

Constantly interlocking
Rings of the rain
Rising deeper and pouring
Into every recess it can gain.

Suddenly the sun breaks through
Brightness abounds
Slowly a ghost of vapour arises
And dry patches secure their ground.

There is a humid calm
A small splash of blue holds onto the grey
The wind is stilled
The storm is away.

MANKIND

Mankind can stand
In the brightest light
Yet can cast the darkest shadow
Quote verse so profound
Yet utter rhetoric
So shallow.

THE WEB

The taught silver threads
Were so carefully spun
With the utmost dexterity
In the early morning sun.

Rainbow colours glistened
From droplets of dew
To a passer-by in a tunnel of jewels
He could not resist flying through.

But Ida the spider
Had weaved her web with great skill
Now Ida was hungry
And poised for the kill.

Although her web was deceivingly cunning
It was beautifully designed and so very neat
But it was purely and simply
There to catch meat.

Total panic the fly hit the trap
The vibrations signalled he was irretrievably stuck
Then on eight fast-moving legs
Ida pounced
And with her venom she struck.

The fly was spun around and around
And wound in a shroud of silk
The little black package paralysed
And bound in a cocoon as white as milk.

Now fastened by the intricate strands
Lies the fly that has run out of luck
And later at her leisure
His life blood she will suck.

TABLE FOR TWO

Table for two
Sitting in the restaurant
The buzz of chatter all around
They sat sipping hot soup in the corner
Never uttering a sound
Their feelings buried deep
Hidden well underneath their mutual frowns.

The young couple next to them
Smiling looking into soft loving eyes
Touching fingertips on the tablecloth
Giggling between the sighs.

Table for two
Listening to secret whispers
Inaudible but envied
None the same
Each one knowing what they had become
Trying to hide the fear, the loss
And the pain.

The clatter of knife and fork
Gave away to the spoon
The sound of coffee cups
Ringing on saucers
Made a mocking
Almost joyful tune.

The young couple
With laughter
Fingers interlaced
The restaurant they vacated
The other two they sat in silence
With their thoughts
Inwardly screaming unabated.

TOPLESS

Down on the hips
Costumes peeled
Pendulous tanned
Breasts revealed.

Some buttocks pert
Others more rotund of cheek
And those that seem to flow
Into thigh so sleek.

A young girl breaks into a wave
With a gasp and a lunge
Hands pressed as in prayer
Shocked by the chill of the plunge.

Wet hair drying in the sun
Around young crowns
Of jet black, blonde,
And chestnut browns.

The sun catches and flares
On a bracelet's silver link
Belonging to a redhead
Foolishly turning pink.

And yet another pair
From out of a warm bra flops
Then onto her beach towel
With her paperback she drops.

She eases her thong
To acquire some slack
Sun lotion glistening
Upon her back.

Whilst an older woman
Now reminiscent
Of those days gone by
When she swam with the dolphins
Under a warm hippy sky.

Cellulite wobbling
Her joints so stiff
The only joint back then
For her was a spliff.

Memories of dancing around a campfire
Gyrating her original hips
Now she shuffles in the shallows
Where she once skinny-dipped.

FIRE BY WATER

Forever moving valley stream
That twines, turns and flows
To polish its countless stones.

Tufts of coarse grass
Overhang the water's edge
With low green blades
While still lies
The splash of flower.

Trees that twist
And grip with roots exposed
Upon the banks
Where a crackling fire glows
Embers dazzling vermillion bright.

In shadows length
Of sinking sun
Leaf-laden boughs
Embrace plaited pillars
Of smoke
Braided and blended
By the invisible wind.

In the gold of evening sky
Flames leap to stab
Eternal space
Until the curtain of the night
Cloaks its dying heart
Leaving silence all around.

Save for the ever-moving
Valley stream
That twines, turns and flows
To polish its countless stones.

CHILDHOOD STREET

When Sunday roast aromas
Filled our neighbourhood street,
There was no sound of running or skipping,
From our childhood feet.

We could not wear old play clothes,
Go fishing for tiddlers in the brook.
So we stuck brightly coloured stamps
Into our Sunday School books.

For calmness dwelt
Upon that Sabbath day,
Dressed in our Sunday best,
Not allowed to run outside and play.

After Sunday dinner
We would build with Meccano,
Do a puzzle or a craft.
If we became too excited,
Dad would say, "Don't act so daft!"

Sunday tea was meat or fish paste
And to fill up your belly,
There was more bread and butter
With tinned fruit and jelly.

Round the open fire,
Sitting in the kitchen,
Weekday tea was bread and jam
And sometimes bread and dripping.

Painted cricket wickets
Upon an old brick wall.
Or two woolly sweaters,
Goal posts to catch the ball.

Those games we played,
There were none better.
Game over,
Pull back on, that holey, woolly sweater.

To run and play, build dens,
Picnic across the fields and the rec.
And to make pea shooters,
From the stems of keck.

With its smells of tobacco
And newspaper print,
Into the corner shop
We would sprint.

For penny chews,
Aniseed balls and liquorice sticks,
Lollipops, gobstoppers,
And sherbet dips.

We carried penknives
And played with matches,
Climbed trees with grazed knees,
Collecting scabs, cuts and scratches.

Yet our childhood
Could have been no better.
Girls tied ropes to gas lampposts
And skipped to 'Salt, mustard, vinegar, pepper'.

Saturday morning minors,
We called the pictures or the flicks.
Cheering at Flash Gordon's sparklers,
Out of a cardboard rocket ship.

Scrumping apples and cherry knocking,
Sword fighting with a stick.
Kiss chase, hide and seek, leapfrog,
Or playing a game of tig.

On those same streets,
Making boots and shoes, factories dwelt.
Producing nuts and bolts, iron and steel,
They did cast, weld and smelt.

Workers with sandwiches and flasks,
In gas mask bags,
The swishing of bicycle spokes.
Demob suits loosely hung
On thin, pale working blokes.

The factory chimneys,
Smoking tall,
The wailing sirens, redundant from war,
But to beckon to work, their eerie call.

Trilbies, caps and bowler hats,
All men for ladies they would doff.
From schoolboys and working men,
To bank managers and the toff.

We listened to Paul Temple on the wireless.
Dick Barton, Jet Morgan and Dan Dare.
We would read our Beanos and Dandys,
Under the table or on the stair.

They were swapped and bartered,
But never sold,
For American comics,
Were just like gold.

Indians whooped, marbles rolled
And cowboys fired cap guns with glee.
Fights broke out over cigarette cards
And once a champion conker belonged to me.

Outside, hop-scotch, chalked on hot summer path.
Dissolved, distorted, streaked by rain.
In the classroom, teachers strict
And stern, but fair,
Backed up with a sturdy cane.

In the corner
The teacher made us stand
When caught in class,
Propelling paper pellets from a rubber band.

Throwing snowballs in the playground,
Sucking icicles and making a slide.
With hot aches in our hands,
When we went back inside.

Parents clipped us round the ear
And sent us all to bed,
When we were found playing doctors and nurses
In our dad's old garden shed.

Boys would snigger
And snicker
At the sight
Of girls in navy knickers.

As girls tossed
Against a wall,
Some modestly tucked in their skirts,
While others just let them fall.

Now Mr Wolf has run out of time,
Queenie has no longer got the ball.
Hide and seek is now replete,
When childhood runs out for us all.

Yet still I smell
The Sunday roasting meat,
Hear the shouts and echoing cries
Of our old childhood street.

Now those kids have grown and flown
To all parts of the globe.
But still its pitted tarmac and old kerbstones
Cling to its timeless road.

STRAY TEAR

I would watch your nipples grow
Beneath your thin-skinned blouse
As many agile fingers
Gently would arouse.

As you enraptured my body with your fragrance
My lips explored every intimate place
And I would ache to dwell longer
In your warm limb-locked embrace.

In the fever of that moment
On my neck you left your mark
Proof in the morning
Of our passion in the dark.

We would bond
Hot between your thighs
Our love cocooned in emotion
That would reflect in your eyes.

Melting silver strings
Wrapped in your delicate wings
Drifting into dreams we would lie
As a lone stray tear
My single eye would cry.

HEATHCLIFF'S WIFE

Rows of smoking
Chimney stacks
Pigeon coops
And chicken shacks.

Washing grey
Upon the line
In cloth cap and boots
Off to the mine.

Heathcliff's wife
Now calls the tune
For she was fed
With a silver spoon.

With Heathcliff dead
She now owns the mine
Alas
For us she has no time.

Misty mornings
Long dark days
Face and hands in coal dust
Lines engraved.

In crystal eye
A teardrop grows
For her
Sherry in cut glass flows.

Her banquets
Spread for dukes and earls
Pale-faced dowagers
Dressed in pearls.

Satin sash
Velvet drapes
Silver service
Wedgewood plates.

Perfumed silks
Expensive furs
And sparkling diamonds
They are hers.

While our children
Kick tin cans in the street
In crude clogs
For their feet.

The grinding wheel
The clanking chain
Pit disasters
Kill and maim.

With choked up lungs
And stinging eyes
Dear old Heathcliff
Hear our cries.

THE WASTE OF WORRY

Upon the brow the furrow ploughed
The seed of worry set
The harvest of your life you lost
Whilst you did needless fret.

FRIENDSHIP

When friendship weighs its anchor
It sails true and free
It is the sturdy vessel
That surrounds you and me.
Time is the ocean
Our lives its ports of call
For those who sail aboard
Their spirits shall never fall.

THE FEAST OF THE FAIRIES

Once in a blue moon in a meadow they would gather
Fairies, elves, goblins and gnomes
Sitting on toadstools in a rainbow of colours
And moss-cushioned fir cones.

Feasting on the roots of mandrake
Elderberries, truffles and hazelnuts
Drinking wolfsbane wine and nightshade ale
From out of acorn cups.

There were bright yellow frogs, scarlet and black
butterflies with Elves dancing with wild abandon
in the fairy ring
A chorus of fairies dressed in purple and gold
Songs of magic and mystery unravelled
As they began to sing.

They were accompanied by a green goblin on a trumpet
And a gnome on a trombone
There was a large buffet on a giant mushroom table
With so much food it began to groan.

For this was the feast of the fairies
In the light of a sapphire blue moon
They supped the nectar of a rare orchid
Through crystal straws and a small silver spoon.

Then some stardust over them was sprinkled
From the hand of a warlock from beneath
The cloak of an ink black sky
Then appeared their guardian the
Elephant hawkmoth
Who had taught them how to fly.

Then they all took off in a flock together
Like a cloud of bats casting shadows over the
sapphire moon
To vanish into the cloak of darkness
To leave a silhouette of the black
Wolf howling his mournful tune.

DIRTY DOGS AND SOUR FLOWERS

The sour flowers work their patch
In all their tack and glitter
A child left alone
She could not find a sitter.

Her dreams are lost but her seams are straight
Her ladders run to a false promised heaven
The hands on her wrist tell her it's time to trade
It's half the hour past seven.

Price fixing through breath steam clouds on thin night air
A raised skirt
A brief kerbstone affair.

Some cash for a quicky
No emotion stirred
A soiled cotton dress
No caress of silk for her.

On pavestones thick stilettos click
In tight top strutting forth once more
Would her next ride be her last?
A phobia for a whore.

A strangler's grip
Striking fear
Would the next request
Be any more strange or queer?

A punter said
As his misty window would downward slide
"Is this your stocking trade?"
Sounding somewhat smug and snide.

Against the lamppost
Legs on display
As young flesh unkindly ages
Then more will drive away.

Flash another slice of flesh
Into the cone of light
Slow down, take another look
Into the depth of loneliness of the night.

Then search and find some fresh young thing elsewhere
Cheap perfume mingles with the sweat
No thought of the future
No past regret.

A prick
A needle shoots heroin or they snort cocaine
Oblivion or ecstasy?
Yet another night of pleasure or pain.

Pull off the petals one by one
Until she wilts and fades
Something burst the stomach churned and curdled
Into the sickening thoughts of AIDS.

Dirty dogs still roam the dark dank streets
And sniff the cold night air
For there is a bunch of sour flowers
Still waiting to be plucked out there.

MIST, SEA AND SHORE

There is a mist upon the sea
And it is a mystery to me
For I am not sure
For I cannot see
Or distinguish
The shore from the sea.

HANDS

They wash the dishes
And set the clocks
Button the shirt
Change the socks.

Yet they can load a gun
And pull the trigger
Or a baby
They can deliver.

They can plant a tree
Or dig your grave
Press together
And pray to be saved.

Tug on the strings of a puppet
To make it dance
Or throw the dice
In a game of chance.

Open the window
Close the door
Perform surgical operations
Or talk with semaphore.

In the handshake of friendship
They can grip
Or on the hilt of a knife
They can thrust and slit.

Gently
They will lay out their dead
Or tenderly
Tuck a child in bed.

Hammer
Or paint and varnish their nails
Or become the eyes
Of a story in Braille.

With arms
They can lovingly embrace
Or with military arms
Destroy another race.

Conduct beautiful music
Pluck at its strings
Or adorn themselves
With tattoos and rings.

They can slap your face
And make you cry
Make love or a cake
Or crumble a pie.

Type a letter
Write a book
Take a coat
Or a fish off the hook.

They can coax
And beckon
Stroke, fight
And threaten.

Point the finger
Wipe a tear from the eye
Applaud the performer
And wave goodbye.

SIT DAD IN THE CORNER

Their father would read them fairy tales
That filled them full of glee
As they snuggled down in bed
Or when they sat upon his knee.

But he would also teach them common sense,
To keep their feet firmly on the ground.
He would clothe and feed them,
And penny pinch to raise his hard-earned pounds.

Their dad was once so young and vibrant
With a full head of dark Brylcreemed hair,
With shiny shoes, a suit and tie,
A trilby hat, he wore with flair.

He would always make them laugh,
He could tell a fantastic tale,
But sit Dad in the corner now,
He's looking wan and pale.

Sit Dad in the corner
Make him comfortable in the chair
With a cup of tea and a custard cream
It seems to take away his vacant stare.

Far behind those rheumy eyes
He lives in his wonderful past
When he was first in the running
When he was never last.

Now his brain is completely addled
Once his mind was as sharp as the proverbial blade
Now they sit him on the veranda
And let him doze in the shade.

A shrivelled husk wrapped in a blanket
He is now all skin and bone
His kids wrapped up in their futures
Have put him in what's ironically called 'a home'.

A few greasy chips with a cardboard pie
That seems to be his main meal
Costing a thousand pounds a week
I think it's what they call a steal.

Now his only friend is his carer
And she's on minimum wage
She's the one that keeps him going
With a cheery smile and a wave.

Time has cruelly taken his youth
You can't believe it was ever there
When he looks beyond you
With that vacant faraway stare.

Sit Dad in the corner
His body is becoming so frail
We don't want a mortality reminder
But now he's looking deathly pale.

"Grandad's fallen asleep, Grandad won't wake up."
They hear the grandchildren say.
"It smells of wee in here,
Can we go out to play?"

Their grandad once read them fairy tales
That filled them full of glee
As they snugged down in bed
Or when they sat upon his knee.

THIRST FOR THE FIRST

Under the merciless disc
Of molten fire,
Aching legs slow to tread
As they start to tire.

Perspiration's salty sting
Runs into eyes from brow
Respite found on an old wooden bench
In the cool of the Cow and Plough.

Apt, that it be a ploughman's lunch,
On a willow-patterned plate.
Underneath a crooked dark-beamed roof
Of ancient thatch and slate.

The noon sun cast through leaded lights,
Reflecting pewter jugs and beaten brass,
Embroidered bubbles of white lace,
Slides slowly down my glass.

Amber beverage of bitter hops,
With top lip froth to soothe my arid tongue,
And so yet, another pint,
So soon it will be gone.

A PUN-NET OF TUTTI FRUTTI

In the land of tutti frutti
The passionfruit ardently loves her date
But her flesh is very cool
The apricots are always stoned
But the gooseberry is no one's fool.

In the land of tutti frutti
Apples are on computers
And bananas stand up straight
And the blackberry likes to ramble
As he leans on the garden gate.

In the land of tutti frutti
The grapes sit on the board
With some big cheese
Where the nuts are the intellectuals
And the pears go around in threes.

In the land of tutti frutti
There is an orange on the phone
And the lemons are really sharp
Unlike the raspberry who popped his cherry
And was caught inside a raspberry tart.

In the underworld of tutti frutti
No one seems to notice
The bitterness of the blackthorn sloes
And in the shadows Victoria plums the depths
Impeached and in fear, where no mangoes.

Deep in the realms of tutti frutti
Oblivious to the slash of red rhubarb wire
That cuts so deep and cruel
There are those that do not give a fig
For their feral damsons still rule.

THE RIGHT TO BEAR ARMS

Let's protect the Second Amendment,
While another child is blown away,
For we have the right to bear arms
In the USA.

She was only six years old,
An innocent bystander, called Suzy,
Brutally she was torn apart,
At close range with an Uzi.

On the campus of a school,
A schizophrenic emptying a full magazine,
Blasting away on a killing spree,
With a blazing M16.

A flash from a rifle muzzle,
A staccato of fire from an Armalite
In a New York suburb,
Creating the dead of the night.

His wife and child,
Would still be alive,
If he had locked down his anger,
And not cocked his Colt Forty-Five.

Between the white and black,
Why is there so much hate?
A young man shot in the back,
With a snubnosed Thirty-Eight.

Macho little men
You imagine you are so much bigger
When you grasp the butt of a gun
And then pull the trigger.

Do you sit on death row?
Pause to think and take stock,
When in that moment of madness,
You took a life with your silver-plated Glock.

He thought it was a toy in an unlocked drawer,
The kid, he knew no better,
He shot and killed his little friend,
With his dad's loaded Beretta.

On the sidewalk he signed his album,
John thought he was a fan,
Then he callously blew him away,
A tragic waste of such a talented man.

I don't wish to remember,
The pathetic shooter's name,
Sadly he thought,
It would bring him notoriety and fame.

So let's protect the Second Amendment,
So more poor souls are blown away,
For we have the right to bear arms
In the USA.

DANDELION

Only a child
Can tell the time
When they blow upon
A dandelion.

Then a thousand airborne fairy seeds
Break forth their dome
'Tis then
The dandelion is sown.

But there are some
Who would malign
That saffron flower
So sublime.

And call it a useless weed
But that beautiful broken globe has flown
When a child's breath is blown
To spread its fertile seed.

HOPE

To lift the spirit
We quote a joke,
Create some laughter
To harness hope.
To be not afraid
To shed the tear,
Learn to cope
And fight the fear.
We roll with the pain
To slacken the strain.
When battle is done
And all is complete,
To then say,
We don't do defeat.
Then we should forget
The stress
And all of the strife,
And make the best
Of the rest of our life.

PANDORA'S BOX

We once put our door keys
Underneath the welcome mat
Or left a window slightly open
To accommodate the cat.

We now have magnetic contact switches
And intricate alarms
Somehow these fortress homes
Have lost their rural charms.

We talk about computers
And all they can achieve
Robots replacing workers
So how can they succeed?

We once breathed in a lungful
Of which we called fresh air
Now with motor car secretions
And ozone depletions we have to take more care.

We did once dream of summer sun
To give us vitamins and tans
Now we worry about melanomas
And going in for scans.

Even the cows are mad, our meat is now malignant
It used to be benign
We changed their names from Buttercup
To BSE, the curse upon the bovine.

For all our complex technology
We have ironically picked the locks
And paradoxically
Opened up Pandora's Box.

THE OLD NOSTALGIA INN

Bring back the old pubs
With a bar and a snug at the rear
Old blokes in cloth caps
Supping mild and bitter beer.

The pub singalongs, those musical modulations
That once filled our ears
Now echo those songs
Throughout the years.

In the lounge bar old ladies in fur coats
And felt hats
Drinking gin and orange
Or rum and blacks.

Young lads full of ale singing in the street
Arms wrapped around the shoulders of beer brothers
Staggering out of one pub
And then on to another.

Crisps, nuts and pork scratchings
Were the standard pub vittles
You might get a ham sandwich after the team had finished
Casting the last cheese at the skittles.

Or a cheese and onion cob
From out of a glass case
Or a chunk of pork pie
Simple fare that would put a smile on your face.

No fine dining
Or haute cuisine
No cappuccino or hot chocolate
With marshmallows and cream
No stacked burgers or French fries
No hint of the American Dream.

Just an eclectic mix
Of tables and chairs
Piles of blazing logs in an inglenook fireplace
That brightly flares.

A farm worker would sit with a well-earned pint
His hands weathered red calloused and rough
From his pocket he would take out a tin
And have a pinch of snuff.

The old pub dog lying under a beer-matted table
Having his daily nap
Old characters laughing, telling jokes and anecdotes
Swigging scrumpy cider on tap.

Back then you could play a game of darts
Pontoon or whist
And not always knowing
When to stick or twist.

Looking for the spots
When it's time to knock nobody knows
Until the flick of the wrist
Then you hear the clicks
When they turn over the dominoes.

Now in the new nostalgia wine bar
The present day young barman
To his customers was about to utter his cliché
"Hi guys, are you dining with us today?"

"No!" said the ghost of yesteryear
Bring back the old pub
With a bar and a snug at the rear
Old blokes in cloth caps
Supping cider and beer.

ENDLESS SOUL

You are the precious jewel
Embedded deep
In the endless ring
That is my soul.

From one seed sown
We became two flowers grown.
Yet still as one
For all time
That nothing can divide.

Yet we are free,
As two eagles
That glide in the wind,
Two leaves,
But one tree.

Two waves,
One ocean.
Two tears,
The same cry,
One emotion.

You are to me
And will always be
The precious jewel
Embedded deep,
In the endless ring
That is the soul.

BLACK MUSHROOMS

Coat collars
Pulled up high
Naked branches
Crack the sky.

Winter bites with frosted teeth
The slicing wind of razor wire
Dashing home
To thaw by an open fire.

Dodging puddles
That encircle feet
Brollies of black mushrooms
Slanted to meet the sleet.

YOUTH'S DELICATE FRAME

Her eyes a misty grey horizon of hope and future growth
The delicate frame of youth
Now that I am older
I see her innocent truth.

Her fragile form carved, curved, slim
Her face pale smooth
As porcelain's slip
Dark clothes in contrast
Flow, drape and grip.

Freckles on her shoulders
Dappled by the sunlight speckled in her
Skin's milky way
Fine soft blonde hair
In neck nape tied away.

Yet one strand falls
To scroll down and spill
To escape
And feed gravity's will.

She walks with an upright grace with conviction
Maturity incarnate
It is a fact
Yet the young fine-hued body can almost defy that.

She talks about her future with expectation
And ambition
The young sapling is set for its fruition.

BROKEN HEART

Love's needle point inflicts its pain
Our broken hearts to bleed
Although its guiding eye is blind
Time's gentle healing thread it weaves
Our broken hearts to bind.

BONES IN A BLANKET

(Ethiopian famine 1984/85)

Bones in a blanket
Lying on a clay floor
Won't see the flies
Round his eyes anymore.

A belly that is empty
Yet ironically blown full
For in our complacency
A nation we cull.

He may be a Marxist
Of which the West can't abide
So don't clothe or feed him
He's not on our side.

When you are shopping for Christmas
And you have eaten your fill
Complain of being bloated
Round the fire from the chill.

Whose birthday party?
Remember that
When you again sit to feed
In your silly paper hat.

Wear it with pride
You Christian soul
For the bones in a blanket
Are tucked away in a hole.

Ham on the bone
Cold turkey for tea
The trivia of trifle
And mince pies for you and for me.

Bones in a blanket
That's covered in dust
Won't share the wishbone
Nor the cast away crust.

Bones in a blanket
Buried beneath a clay floor
Won't see the flies
Round his eyes anymore.

THE SOUND OF THE SEA

Surf stirs and swirls the fine seaweed
Clinging to the surface of a scallop's shell
To see it shine in the soft smooth sand
As it's soaked by the ocean's salty swell.

EYEWITNESS

Someone watched Rome burn
With the Emperor Nero
A Sistine Chapel assistant
Painting with Michelangelo
A model from the street
Painted in shadow by Caravaggio
A ghost writing on the dark side
With Edgar Allan Poe
A fellow performer in the circus
With the clown Coco
Many appeared on screen
With Marilyn Monroe
Or pitching and catching
With Joe DiMaggio
Boxing in rings
With Rocky Marciano
Many were there
When Kennedy and Onassis
Both married Jackie O
The Experience with Jimi Hendrix
When he sang 'Hey Joe'
The break-up of The Beatles
And Yoko Ono
The shooting of John Lennon
Oh no! Oh no!

BUTTERFLY IN THE RAIN

Once your wings were so colourful and bright
Now dull and ragged as you take flight
You know not your destination
Yet you try to escape in desperation.

You were dashing helter-skelter
Desperately seeking shelter
But the moment your wings were torn
You could not outrun the storm.

Now I understand your pain
Butterfly battered in the rain
Once you would dance in the dazzling sun
Now I sadly watch your colours run.

Now lies a delicate broken rainbow
From which life ebbs and drains
As I watch your colours running
Running in the rain.

DEALER

Hoody cowled,
Head down bent,
Wagging thumbs,
Message sent.

Headphones full,
Of loud rap,
At a burger van,
Eating crap.

Black tight jeans,
Baggy top,
Dirty trainers,
Off he trots.

Small plastic bag,
Deal is done,
In damp dark alley,
Reached not by the sun.

Cops arrive,
One fat one lean,
Too late,
The snowman's melted,
From the scene.

NATURE'S CROWNING GLORY

In spring when nature wears
Her floral crown
Bright petals splashed
Upon fresh green ground.

She endeavours to paint
Her vast canvas of earth and sky
Where nature's bold palette
Is never shy.

From meadows to hedgerows
Flowers thrust through in stem-crushed crowds
And tree blossoms burst
To compete with cumulus clouds.

Summertime when nature wears
Her crown of gold
To mirror the sun
To cast out the cold.

The curvature of the Earth distorted
In a shimmering haze
Reflecting the mirage of a quicksilver horizon
On long hot summer days.

Under tree-cast cool shadows
Where sheep and cattle lie
To gaze across a field of saffron yellow
And watch the erratic flight of a dancing butterfly.

An autumn day slowly breaks
Upon a mist dull dawn
Summer's past green pastures scorched
Corn crop fields plough-torn.

Nature now wears
Her copper crown
And paints a more mature landscape
Of old gold, burnt sienna, red and brown.

When winter's last rust-coloured leaves
Leave the trees
With a final rustling whisper
From a chilling breeze.

The cold bitter air
Now void of the buzzing of insects and bees
Rooks flapping their black ragged wings
As they roost and caw in those naked trees.

It's then that nature
Dons her silver crown
As the frost embraces
The frozen ground.

THE HIGHWAYMAN

I was a highwayman,
I was known as a rogue,
But I dressed like a dandy,
When I robbed from the road.

I drank at the taverns,
Made merry in the inns of the town,
Where I was hunted by the Bow Street Runners,
In the name of the Crown.

With a brace of pistols,
Primed ready to hand,
On my black stallion,
I would order the coach to stand.

I robbed from the rich,
Bought bread and ale for the poor,
I spent the rest,
On gambling, drinking and whores.

Now in Newgate Prison,
Awaiting my trial,
They will tell of my crimes,
Paint a picture so vile.

So off in the wagon,
To stand in the shadow of Tyburn's tree,
A short life and a wild one,
That was for me.

I'll call in every ale house,
On my way to my doom,
I'll tell jokes and tell tales,
In their dark dingy rooms.

Like Dick Turpin and Jack Sheppard,
I hope it's swift and not slow,
Then off for some air dancing,
I will merrily go.

To some I was a hero,
To others a rogue,
I slept in the brothels,
And robbed from the road.

I kissed ladies' hands,
I made them all swoon,
Then I took their jewellery,
And vanished, as a shadow across the full moon.

I was a highwayman,
I would make you shake and quiver,
Then I would demand,
You stand and deliver.

I once would fill you with fear,
I would fill you with dread,
Now 'tis I that hang,
On a creaking rope, now dead.

Now 'tis limp I dangle,
On the gallows tree,
My body be dead,
But my soul not free.

My bones in a gibbet,
Food for the crows,
Now my ghost rides on the crossroads,
Where no one dare go.

THE PASSING

Youth in your springtime beauty
Know not the call of autumn's sting
October chill that shall entwine me
And finally
Winter's cold blast of wind
A pure white shade of death.

But fear not
For mortal man dwells not with me
But within my soul
Ego, take flight be free
For to know not nor care
But just to be.

BORN TO BE MILD

My name is mild Phil Hickok
And I'm into the Western scene
Although I've never been to Tombstone
Dodge City or Abilene.

The furthest west I have been
Is Weston-super-Mare
And you don't find many bandits
Or desperadoes there.

I have never been in a barroom brawl
Or done anything remotely risky
Like chasing wild women, gambling
Or drinking rotgut whiskey.

I have never ridden a bucking bronco
Or lassoed and branded a cow
Never ridden bareback on a Palomino stallion
I just would not know how.

I have never slid a full beer glass
Along a barroom counter
Or spit on the saloon's dusty wooden floor
Never rushed in with six guns blazing
After kicking in the jailhouse door.

I have never owned a pair of silver spurs
Or had stubble upon my chin
Never worn a hat with a snakeskin band
Or perfected a crooked grin.

I have never been in a bordello
With a cheroot dangling off my lip
Never dressed all in black
A pearl-handled peacemaker
Strapped to my hip.

Never put powder and shot in a long-barrelled musket
Or stood defiantly on the walls of The Alamo
In buckskins and a raccoon skin hat
Or rode the Chisholm Trail
And fried pork and beans in buffalo fat.

I have never ridden shotgun for Wells Fargo
And fired a Winchester Seventy-Five
Never had my face on a poster
With a large reward 'Wanted, Dead or Alive'.

You see I have never been an outlaw
And leapt from my horse onto a fast-moving train
Never rode through the night to escape the posse
In a poncho in the driving wind and the rain.

Never formed a circle with a wagon train
Or stood back-to-back with George Armstrong Custer
Fighting off the Indian horde
Trying to repel the whole Sioux nation
With a hot Colt Forty-Five and a
Broken cavalry sword.

But I do like to dream
While I play my Country and Western
And on a Wednesday
I go to line dancing class
And when I get home I open the sherry
But I only have the one glass.

FIRST LIGHT

A shadow cast on curtain
Bright from dark
Early birdsong
A dog lets loose its bark.

Milk bottles rattle
On float that groans
Postman's feet
On gravel stones.

Alarm clock ticking
About to ring
The kettle in the kitchen
Starts to sing.

Against the top sheet
I curl my toes
As coffee and toast fumes
Pleasantly pervade my nose.

ALCOHOL, MY ENEMY OR MY FRIEND?

Like an innocent stream
You flow
Seeds of merriment
You first sow.

Then beyond
The threshold deep
Into man's soul
You start to seep.

Causing more
To pass his lips
Bulbous nose
Shaking fingertips.

Liquid beverage
Sweet and sour
For youth
You do deflower.

Wine so potent
Beer so cold
To parched palettes
You are sold.

Countless throats
You do pass
Turn sensible men
Into many an ass.

Yet for this
You wicked brew
We cannot help
But all love you.

Beer of plenty
Port and wine
Pass my lips
Many a time.

Some sing some laugh
Some shout aloud
Just a happy
Drinking crowd.

Drunks start to sway
People want to stay
Have another drink
Forget their day.

Then your name
In vain I take
Yet I know
It is but a fickle hate.

The staircase
That seems so steep
The spinning room
In which I try to sleep.

Finally unconscious and dribbling
In a fitful snoring doze
Uttering guttural noises
Through my mouth and nose.

Heavy lays your head
Next morn
As you awake wishing
You had never been born.

Then it is said
Without much doubt
A hair of the dog
Keeps despair out.

But what of demon drink they say
No! It is my friend I'm sure
For tomorrow
Shall I not drink more?

THE REMNANT OF LIFE

The delicate cloth
The complex pattern
The threads from which we hang
Yet still we this fabric weave
This yarn we spin
The gauze draped across our path
The unseen blanket
One day will lift
To show our naked truth
Then time
Like a moth
Will eat away our weaving stitch
To reveal an empty space
We call eternity.

SLEEP

My eyelids fluttered
And settled
Like two nesting birds.

Then my eyes sank
Like two stones
Into the deep warm pool
Of dreams.

Where I saw a myriad
Of coloured pictures
Then my eyes
Floated like two corks.

Bobbing in my head
On the bright surface
Of morning.

THE SUN OF VESTA AND RA

Vesta's scarlet flame burns eternal
As Ra rides her blood red clouds
Their sun falls to Earth and appears to sink into
Horizon's tomb
But its birth is conceived
As it sets into the western womb.

Then day lifts horizon's eastern skirts of night
And the morning midwife attends the pregnant dawn
To her another sun is born
And all is true to form
In the age-old start of day
Where Vesta's scarlet flame burns eternal
As Ra rides the blood red clouds away.

LOVE BIRDS

I will pluck your pink tulips
And open up the petals
And make your stamen cry
Then let the love birds hover
To dip, sip and fly.

You will take away my nectar
With my pollen on your wings
And your honey on my bill
I will then leave you
In your warm dewed beauty
When we have supped our fill.

Then when it comes to summer
Heavy-laden your blossom bough
Let the seed once more
Be scattered
And I will have been your plough.

TRUMP 2018

The past scandals of the war crimes
In the prison of Abu Ghraib
For the US and the Stars and Stripes
It most certainly did degrade.

Now we have Trump
And our disbelieving minds are in a whirl
Alas he's now the leader
Of the so-called 'free world'.

The Western world has been taken over
By the absurd world of Trump
I hope the senate will soon impeach him
Then this abomination they can dump.

It causes me so much worry
For sanity I grieve
But I suppose Vladimir Putin
Is laughing up his sleeve.

In his past there was so much scandal and sleaze
I can't believe he won the vote
This crotch-grabbing clown
This moron Don is way past a joke.

A misogynist
A creator and a faker of fake news
So watch out world
For honest people will get screwed.

His hair is so ridiculous
In a never-ending orange quiff
With a name like Trump it would suggest
He leaves behind a rather nasty whiff.

He's narcissistic, egotistic, a megalomaniac
He's also alas
Arrogant, inarticulate
Dangerous and crass.

He is unbelievable, the depth of his
Ignorance is so vast
He now wants to introduce weapons
For teachers in the class.

He's a bully and a yob
He's totally void of any class
And as his name would suggest
He talks out of his arse.

In the USA you can't drink alcohol
Until you are twenty-one
But at the age of eighteen
You can go out and buy a gun.

They call the United States
The land of the free
Tell that to the Native Americans
And the black community.

Some leaders build bridges
Others they build walls
While the former connects with other nations
The latter in time they all must fall.

MOON BEACH

Full-faced
Or crescent-veiled
Endlessly you tug the tide
And stir the sea
To break
Foam-crocheted lace
Upon the shore.

Your distorted image
Briefly stretched
In polished sand
The jagged rocks
Struggling in waves crest
Grinding down
Spume broken
In endless rows
To rise and yield
Until the end of time.

Disappearing footprints
Surround a child's castle
The fantasies of day
Diminished
The fortress walls
Breached in flooding brine
Left cone hewn
Worn and dull.

A paper flag sags
Then spins away
In the tide's swirling motion
Lost in the moonlit spray.

Clouds hide your face
You seem wistful, shy
Soon in full gold
You will bloom
Then boldly glide into view
Endlessly to tug the tide
And stir the sea.

WHEN

When did we stop listening to comedy on a wooden wireless,
To make us laugh?
When did we stop to wonder
How many kettles did it take to fill a tin bath?

When did we stop sparking Blakeys
On our worn out shod feet?
When did the Bobby
Stop calming traffic on his beat?

When kids gathered on fog-filled street corners,
You would hear a familiar cry,
When they would ask for a penny
For their perambulated Guy.

When did we stop swinging
On the old cast iron lampposts?
When did we stop eating sugar sandwiches,
Or dripping on toast?

When was the last time
We bought a bar of Fruit and Nut for a tanner?
When did we stop tightening our Meccano nuts
With a minute rusty red spanner?

What happened to icicle-hung winters of bitter cold?
When ebonised dusty men
Delivered sacks of nutty slack,
Coke and coal.

What happened to tar-melting summers
So scorching hot?
When the only sound was the murmur of bees,
In harmony with the humming of a child's spinning top.

The memory of the smell, of the baker's bread basket,
When he delivered on our street.
The kids in short trousers,
With pink chapped legs, in the rain and the sleet.

What became of the old cobbler,
Working in his leather-filled shop?
Was it then,
When working men's whistling stopped?

RAINBOW SPLINTERS

Clear is the harsh cold sky,
The moon brass bright,
Still and bitter lies
The frozen night.

Needles of frost upon the grass,
In midnight's brittle winter,
Walking on broken glass,
Crunching prisms of rainbow splinters.

In reflecting lunar light icicles weep,
As crystals slowly grow,
Dripping droplets penetrate deep,
In drifting powdered snow.

Then the full moon fades,
From gold to white,
To give the new-born day,
The vanquished night.

Silver webs bounce on a skeletal bush,
As a blast of bleak wind blows,
Pale gold sunlight, a Midas touch,
On the weathered, withered hedgerows.

The morning's twisting mist,
A clouded cloak across the sun,
Then ascends the scarlet disc,
At last, the rime of night is done.

THE FORTUNES AND FOLLIES OF FAME

To ride the wild horse of ambition,
Straddle the saddle of fame,
Bask in the beam of the spotlight,
To embrace that eternal flame.

To hear the theatre's deafening applause,
Of appreciation,
In the stadium, thousands unseated,
To a standing ovation.

The roar of the crowd,
In adulation,
Then the craving for privacy,
You seek in desperation.

To escape, leap into the abyss of addiction,
Indulge in the hedonistic game,
Then, into rehab to play the clean ethical hero,
To shrug off the mantle of shame.

Now, in reclusive sobriety,
Respectability so sublime,
Your star now cast in the sidewalk,
Thousands of autographs signed.

Memoirs, written in reflective seclusion,
Over the passing decades,
Icons now immortalised,
For others, fame eventually fades.

And finally, to walk down the red carpet,
To claim the long-awaited Oscar of gold,
While vanity massages the ego,
To find you have lost your soul.

IT'S COOL

It's cool to drink out of a bottle
To drive while on the phone
To aspire to be a waif-like model
To be all skin and bone.

It's cool to wear designer labels
That cost an arm and a leg
To worship the latest celebrity
To envy their car's personalised reg.

It's cool to blast your eardrums with the latest music
With your baseball cap on back to front
To mumble to your parents
Or just to nod and grunt.

It's cool to have a navel piercing
Or a butterfly tattooed on the cheek of your bum
To split the knees of your jeans
And wear a silver ring on your thumb.

It's cool to have a bare midriff in winter
And to show off the top of your thong
To drink Tequila Slammers
And have a stud through your nose or your tongue.

But I wonder twenty years in the future
How cool to you it will seem
You will perhaps look back with a wry smile
And it will appear to have been a dream
That's cool.

SUMMER'S DOOR

Pewter clouds
Sullen lie
On hills' solemn brow
Blackbirds snatch
Berries bright
From Rowans
Autumn Bough.

Leaves cascade
In many shades
To carpet
The forest floor
Russet red and gold
They swirl
To close
Summer's door.

TRANQUIL SHADOWS

May you always stand in the light,
Yet tranquil shadows be yours to command,
Let destiny guide you beside still waters,
Reap the ripe harvest of knowledge
And know the true beauty of life.